ECONSENSE

Economics for Everyday Living

Wes Clark

innovativeink
PUBLISHING
A Division of Kendall Hunt

Cover image Wes Clark

innovativeink
PUBLISHING
A Division of Kendall Hunt

www.innovativeinkpublishing.com
Send all inquiries to:
4050 Westmark Drive
Dubuque, IA 52004-1840

Print ISBN: 979-8-3197-1619-4
eBook ISBN: 979-8-3197-1620-0

Published in the United States of America

Contents

INTRODUCTION v

CHAPTER 1: Basics of Economics 1

CHAPTER 2: Economic Market Systems 9

CHAPTER 3: Markets: Supply and Demand 17

CHAPTER 4: Market Failures 23

CHAPTER 5: Introduction to the Macroeconomy 29

CHAPTER 6: Macroeconomic Theory 35

CHAPTER 7: Fiscal Policy 39

CHAPTER 8: What is Money? 43

CHAPTER 9: Monetary Policy 49

CHAPTER 10: Consumer Actions 53

CHAPTER 11: Production Cost 57

CHAPTER 12: Industry/Market Structures 61

CHAPTER 13: Resources 65

CHAPTER 14: Last Thoughts 69

Introduction

Over my 12 years as a professor of economics and more importantly my 35 years in business, I have seen that much of the population knows very little about the discipline of economics. Economic classes are known for their math, graphs, and overall difficulty level, with good reason. I have had students tell me it is like studying a foreign language. My goal over the last 10 years has been to make sure students taking my principles of economics classes can not only know and understand the concepts but be able to apply economic concepts as well.

Out of this pursuit, I started trying to open the subject to more people. I started a podcast in 2022 called EconSense (which can be found on Spotify, Apple Podcast and now YouTube) in the hopes of reaching more people and helping them understand economics. This book is the continuation of that goal. I hope you find it easy to read and understand, ultimately leading you to want to explore the discipline even more.

If that is the case, I recommend seeking material from Dr. Thomas Sowell, whom has had a huge impact on my career, and I believe to be one of the most brilliant people to live in the last few hundred years. He has many videos, columns, and books to help you explore economics.

I dedicate this book to him, my family, my friends, and my students. I hope you enjoy.

Wes Clark
wes.the.economist@gmail.com
@westheeconomist on Facebook, Instagram and X.
EconSense Podcast – Spotify, Apple and Youtube
jc

1 Basics of Economics

The first question I ask my class every semester is, “What do you think economics is about?” The first answer that always gets called out is, “Money.” My students are always surprised to hear that economics is not really about money, though we do talk extensively about it. Economics, at its heart, is the study of why people make the choices they do with their resources in times of scarcity. Regrettably, economic knowledge throughout our society has steadily been going in the wrong direction. My hope is that this book will help bring some economic sense back in a basic form. Economics is fundamentally about common sense, and it does not take a college degree to understand. Within these pages, I want to break economics down in a very simple manner with the hope that afterwards, you will be enticed to study more about the subject.

Economics

As I stated previously, the study of economics is the study of why people make choices with their resources in times of scarcity. Resources have many potential uses; therefore, choices must be made about what to do with them. Every time a choice is made, something is given up; this is an opportunity cost. Opportunity cost can be defined in several different ways. It can be looked at as the cost of one decision resulting in the loss of the ability to make a different decision. Another way is to state that the cost of a decision is the price of the next optimal decision. There are a limited number of resources in any scenario; however, there are unlimited wants in each of those same scenarios. There are many things that we would like to have, but our limited resources do not allow us to obtain them.

This does not mean there are right and wrong decisions, just the realization that every choice has a cost associated with it. The time you are taking to read this book could be spent doing something else, including working and bringing home a wage. You could also be spending time at the beach, watching a movie, or reading a different book. Once you have used the time to read this book, you will never be able to use that time for anything else (I hope you find the time well worth it). As we progress through this book, you will find that the concept of opportunity cost is an underlying foundation of most economic reasoning.

Resources

When economists look at resources, we tend to break them into very general categories. As you continue further into the subject, these generalizations can become more specific depending on the subject matter we are tackling. At first, we put them into the broad groups of natural resources, labor, capital, and entrepreneurship.

Sometimes, a natural resource is simply labeled as land, but it can be anything that comes from nature that is used in the economic process. This can range from land itself to air, water, gold, petroleum, diamonds, wood, and so forth. If it occurs in nature, then we classify this as a natural resource or land resource.

Labor is exactly as it sounds. This is the resource of work, the outcome of your time in any given endeavor. This does not include the entire population, just those in the labor force. In a broader scope, we look at the labor force inside of a society, which includes the people who are looking for work or who are working in that country.

As soon as you hear the word capital, I am sure you immediately think of money. Yet capital is any product that is made and then used in the production of another good or service. It is actually not money; the reason we associate it with money is that usually when a company raises "capital", it usually talks about dollar amounts. But think about what companies do with that "capital"; they usually go and purchase equipment to run their business. Hence, the real meaning of capital is the man-made products used in producing goods and services.

The final resource is entrepreneurship. This is usually defined as someone who starts a small business, which is correct in the sense that it takes entrepreneurship to take that risk. But entrepreneurship is much bigger than that; it also occurs in corporations. Entrepreneurship is the ability to arrange the first three resources in new and innovative ways by producing new products or better products. In fact, one of the best examples of entrepreneurship can be traced back to a significantly large corporation. Apple, in the last 60 years, has literally changed no less than three industries. The first being the computer industry with the introduction of the first Macintosh. The innovation was not that it was a personal computer, but that they used what is called a GUI or graphical user interface known as the Finder. That, along with the included mouse, changed the way we did computing. Apple also changed the cell phone industry. When the iPhone was introduced, cell phones were getting smaller. After its introduction, we saw phones getting bigger, but more importantly becoming small computers that could be taken anywhere. These were significant innovations, but the biggest innovation would be iTunes. iTunes along with the iPod completely changed how we bought, stored, and listened to music. It basically changed the entire pricing structure of the music industry. None of these "Innovations" were new products. They merely took what already existed and made it into better products.

We will see in the coming sections how these resources fit into the scheme of economics. Remember, economics is the study of how we use our resources, or land, labor, capital, and entrepreneurship. There are many competing uses of these resources, and each time a choice is made, the opportunity to make another choice is gone.

Branches of Economics

Economics is usually broken down into two distinct branches, each looking at a different aspect of society. The first branch is microeconomics, and as designated by its prefix, it looks at the small parts. The second one is macroeconomics, which, as designated by its prefix, looks at the bigger picture.

Microeconomics examines the individual units of the economy such as individuals, individual businesses, individual markets, and theories about how these individual units make decisions. It is like watching a football game and paying close attention to each facet of the game. What type of play is the offensive running against a certain defense? What is the defense doing between each play? What is happening with the field conditions? What are the strategies that both teams are following to try to win the game? And I could continue indefinitely. The idea is that you are looking at the individual pieces of the game or picture to see what is happening underneath.

Macroeconomics looks at everything in one picture, aggregating all aspects of the economy into one entity. We look at things that affect the economy as a whole, such as unemployment, inflation, gross domestic product, government, and other items that tell the story of the whole. Using the football game to illustrate this, we will be just sitting, enjoying the game as it unfolds from the larger view. We are concerned with the score and who has the ball, but we are looking at all the other small pieces as one picture.

Most economists can come to an agreement on the micro topics of economics, with a few exceptions. However, when it comes to looking at the macro topics, there is much more debate and, frankly, fights over how the individual units work together. We will explore some of these divisions as we go through this book.

Defining the Economic Issues of People in Society

While we go through the study of economics, I will try to stay away from math and graphs since so many people have an aversion to them. However, there are some topics that are more easily explained with graphs and formulas.

The first situation we want to look at is an issue that most people face: having a budget but also having a lot of wants in their life. In economics, this is called a budget constraint model, meaning we only have so much money, which we obtained from one of our resources, to be able to buy the things that we need and the things that we want. We must make a choice on what we are going to use our money for, therefore the choices for which our resources are traded. So, we could either buy a quantity of item A or a quantity of item B; choices have to be made with our limited resources. For each quantity of what we choose, we give up a certain quantity of the other item and vice versa. This goes back to the opportunity cost of a decision. Another way to look at it is that there is a trade-off between A and B. We speak of this in terms of product for product and not money, because from an economic point of view, the trade-off is not about how much money you spent but how much of A was given up for B or how much of B was given up for A.

Let's look at a real-life example. If I go into a local fast-food restaurant with $10 in my pocket, I must look at the products on the menu and decide which one will bring me more satisfaction if I buy it. Also, do I want to buy more than one product with my budget of $10? For each item I choose to buy, I have given up the opportunity to buy a different product on the menu, or there has been a trade-off between those products as I made that choice. There is no right or wrong choice; it all comes back to what will bring me the most satisfaction when consuming. The economic principle here again is that there has been a trade-off with my choice. In other words, we are examining why someone has made this choice with his or her resources in a time of scarcity.

I should note here where that $10 came from, so that we can see the tie-in with the resources and not the money itself. For most of us, we work for any money that we spend, or at least maybe someone gave us that money from the fruits of their labor. So, there is the key, someone has traded labor for $10 and then we take that $10 and we buy something that we want. We are studying the choices that people make with their resources, in this case, labor.

Now this is a very oversimplified example of a much more complex issue; however, by understanding this simple model, it becomes easier to understand the more complex issue of having a paycheck and out of all the products we can consume, which ones will we choose. In a later chapter, we will look at something called consumer behavior in which we analyze why people make the choices they make based on their preferences. Now let's move on to society as a whole.

Production Possibility Model

This same thought pattern can be applied to an overall societal issue. What can we produce in a given economy based on our allotment of resources? Our resources being natural resources, labor, capital, and entrepreneurship. Every society has a certain allotment of these resources, and its members must decide how they are going to use them. We can only use what we have at a certain time with the technology available. The combination of these resources put together in certain ways will give us the possibilities of what products we can put out. Again, we will oversimplify this example to show you how this would work in a more complex situation.

As before, we will look at item A and item B. We will say that all society can only produce so much of each item, or some combination in between. Just as in the budget constraint model, we will use the idea that for every time we make a choice, we give up the opportunity of using our resources to make another item and vice versa. Just as in the individual model, as a society, we must make the choices about how much of item A we will make and how much of item B. Again, we will look at the trade-offs in terms of each other, when we make item A, we give up the opportunity to make item B and when we make item B, we give up the opportunity to make item A. So, opportunity cost and trade-offs again show us that there is a price for using our resources to make certain items.

Circular Flow Model

Now let's look at putting our economy together, and again, we will start with a very simple model that only includes businesses and households. This model shows the sale of resources and the sale of products. Households control all the resources and sell them in the resource market; they become factors of production for businesses to buy. The businesses take the resources and convert them into goods and services and sell them in the product market where households purchase them.

The first thought is, what about the resources the companies own? If you break down companies, you will soon see that households control these also. In a sole proprietorship, the one owner controls all the company's resources. In a partnership, two or more people will control these resources and, in a corporation, the shareholders own the company, who in turn own resources the corporation has as assets. These individuals are the households, so households own all resources, even if it is through having shares in a corporation.

Now looking at the other side of the model, there must be something that allows businesses to buy resources from households and households to buy products from businesses. This is where money comes in. Money is just a tool that we use to change our resources into products that we want. Households have expenditures on products that become revenue to businesses. At that point, businesses must pay the cost for resources, which become income to households. We can break down the income into the payment for the resources, for natural resources - rent is paid, for labor - wages are paid, for capital - interest is paid, and for entrepreneurship - profit is paid. (We will look at this in more detail when we talk about gross domestic product later in the book). One interesting point here is that most people assume when the company makes a profit, they keep it, but in reality, it is either reinvested in the company or paid to the owners.

Overall, this is just a way to see how resources are sold and become factors of production before they are made into goods and services sold to households. This is called the real flow. The other side is called the money flow and it's just payment for goods and services and resources with whatever money type is used in society. But once again the money is just a tool for people to convert their resources into the products they want or for businesses to convert their product into resources they use for production.

This is the simplest circular flow model because it only has firms and households. To expand it, we must also include the government which interacts with the resource and product market as well as regulates and taxes businesses and households. We also must add international dealings, in which people around the world sell and buy resources and sell and buy products in the product market. This is beyond the scope of this book and, suffice it to say, we are exploring the basics; giving an oversimplified model, so the more complex can be understood.

Discussion Questions

1. **Economics is often described as the study of choice under scarcity rather than the study of money.** Why do you think people commonly associate economics with money, and how does the chapter's definition change the way you think about everyday decisions?
2. **Opportunity cost is described as what you give up when you make a choice.** Can you think of a recent personal decision where the opportunity cost was not money, but something else like time, experiences, or future options?
3. **The chapter identifies four types of resources: natural resources, labor, capital, and entrepreneurship.** Choose a common product you use every day and explain how all four resources might be involved in producing it.
4. **Microeconomics focuses on individual decision-making, while macroeconomics looks at the economy as a whole.** Why do you think economists tend to agree more on microeconomic issues than macroeconomic ones?
5. **In the circular flow model, money is described as a tool rather than a resource itself.** How does this idea change the way you think about earning income and spending it in the economy?

2 Economic Market Systems

Market Systems

How do all these concepts work together in an economy? Well, there are two extreme forms of market systems: the free market and the command market. After researching them, we find that most nations fall somewhere in between the two, with a mix of free and command elements.

Let's first examine the three main questions of economics: What will be produced? How will it be produced? Who will be able to have the product? We will explore these questions for both extremes of the market systems. More importantly, we will assess the mix of the two to distinguish which countries lean more towards a free market and which ones tend towards a command market.

This analysis is straightforward in a command system. A central entity, be it the government or another body, owns all the resources. They decide what will be produced; all goods and services are determined by a central planning entity. They also decide how goods and services will be produced, including the techniques and procedures used. Moreover, they dictate who will be able to buy or obtain the products. In these rare economies, no decisions are made by the population. Presently, only two countries employ this economic system: Cuba and North Korea.

In a free economy, this analysis becomes more intricate, the population is answering these questions, meaning there is no central decision-making process to observe. In the next chapter, we will see how the population actually allocates resources for products through markets.

In a free market, what will be produced is determined by what people are willing to buy with the money they earn from utilizing their resources. Companies strive to find products that people are willing to buy and that they can sell for a profit. Profit seems to have acquired a negative connotation in our society, but if we reflect on the circular flow model, any profits made ultimately flow back to individuals, specifically the owners of the company. People don't invest money expecting only to get their capital back; they anticipate a return on their investment. The higher returns on the investment, the more likely funds will be available for the venture. However, usually the higher the return the more risk the investor will have to take.

In a free market, all decisions are made within society. What will be produced? Items that people are willing to buy. How will it be produced? Firms will produce at the lowest possible cost, enabling people to acquire items at a low price. Some argue that this might lead to the production of cheap products. However, if a company intends to stay in business, it cannot afford to sell a product that doesn't meet consumers' expectations. Continuous disappointment in product quality would deter people from buying, leading to the demise of the business. Who will receive the product? In a free market, it will be those who can afford to buy it.

The primary argument against a free-market today is that it is driven by greed. In the words of the renowned economist Milton Friedman, "Is there some society...that doesn't run on greed?"[1] What Dr. Friedman emphasized is that all systems involve some form of self-interest. In a free market, money-driven greed exists, but in a command market, there is a greed for power and, in some cases, fame. The pursuit of various desires is the motivation. The critical question becomes which system is the best choice. When we examine empirical evidence, no other system has allocated resources more efficiently or aided more people than a free market. Yes, this is considered capitalism, but it's crucial to understand that the United States has not practiced true capitalism in a long time. People today claim that capitalism inevitably results in large companies, which is contrary to the essence of a free market. In a free market where competition thrives, any substantial corporation is eventually overtaken by an

1. Milton Friedman, interview by Phil Donahue, *The Phil Donahue Show*, television program, NBC, 1979.

innovative newcomer with a superior idea and a more efficient use of resources (Entrepreneurship).

If you haven't discerned it yet, this section is discussing capitalism versus socialism. I deliberately avoided using these terms because they have become highly politicized. However, as an economist, they are purely economic concepts to me, signifying who controls the resources, either in terms of ownership or allocation. I won't assert that free markets are flawless; no system is perfect. If a perfect system emerges, I'd be more than willing to celebrate its merits. Until then, I will side with the first economist, Adam Smith, who maintained that through free markets, society prospers. Decisions made by individuals in the market to safeguard their self-interest inadvertently enhance the entire economy. Not because participants in the free market intend to do so, but through the allocation of their resources, their self-interest ultimately benefits everyone. He termed this phenomenon "the invisible hand," denoting choices made in the economy that guide us towards efficiency.

Echoes from the last financial crisis still resonate, with mentions of companies deemed "too big to fail." If we've reached a point where companies are too big to fail, we are no longer in a free market; we have deviated into something distorted that merely resembles a free market. And in economic terms, we are heading towards a command market. Maybe not the government owning resources, but controlling what can be produced, how it is produced and who will receive it by passing laws and regulations.

Consider North and South Korea, regions that began with similar resources approximately 70 years ago but have evolved into two vastly different societies. One, barely surviving, is under a command system, while the other, flourishing, is based on a free market system. I could dedicate an entire book to this topic alone, but we must move forward.

Observing all countries, one realizes that there is no genuinely free market existing on the planet. Nearly all economies are some form of mixed market, blending elements of free markets and government intervention. (We will delve deeper into this in a subsequent chapter.) The next challenge is to gauge how free or command-oriented a market is. Several methods can accomplish this. For our discussion, I will outline a few characteristics that can be used to assess economies on a scale.

The first characteristic is private property, extending beyond land. More broadly, it encompasses all resources. Are individuals permitted to use their resources as they see fit? If the answer is yes, it indicates a free market. Are individuals free to pursue any job they desire with the proper training? Can they utilize their land in any way and sell their natural resources? With access to capital, can they invest in any type of business? Are they free to use their entrepreneurial skills to develop new ideas? In the United States, we would argue that we have this freedom for most of these aspects. Let's scrutinize this more closely, focusing on land as an example.

Can landowners use their land for any purpose they wish? Well, naturally, there are sensible limitations that prevent harm to others in the vicinity. Setting these aside, can landowners employ their land in ways that benefit them and society? Often, this is contingent on the land's location. In rural areas, there are fewer restrictions on land use, although there might be some local zoning constraints. As you progress into counties with more control, it becomes evident that your freedom diminishes. Numerous instances abound of people being dictated on what their buildings should look like and how they should construct them on their private land. This applies not only to land but to other resources as well; are individuals permitted to utilize their resources as they wish? Do you even actually own property anymore, since if you do not pay your property taxes, you could lose your property.

This leads us to the freedom of choice. Are individuals at liberty to purchase what they desire or embark on the enterprise they wish to pursue? For the most part, the United States grants considerable freedom in these areas. However, starting a business nowadays isn't simple. There are numerous governmental hurdles one must overcome to establish a legitimate business. In other countries, it's even more challenging, sometimes reaching the point of corruption, with governments dictating what individuals can or cannot do. I have a friend who visited Cuba a few years ago; she lives in Nicaragua, making it convenient for her to vacation in Havana. Despite Nicaragua's shortcomings concerning freedom, when it comes to enterprise, it's far more lenient than Cuba. She recounted an incident where she was waiting for eggs one morning for breakfast. The inn where she was staying had to wait for a shipment from outside the city. She observed plenty of chickens and numerous eggs to choose from around the area. However, the government had decreed that only eggs from specific farms could be sold within the city. Even though people owned chickens, they were forbidden from selling the eggs they produced to those around them.

Another characteristic to consider is self-interest, an idea Adam Smith outlined in his book, *The Wealth of Nations*[2]. Allowing people to look out for their own self-interest means they can determine what is best for themselves. This doesn't necessarily imply selfishness, although some individuals can be exceptionally self-centered. Let's face it, when you receive your paycheck, your concern is to take care of what's best for you, not relinquishing your entire paycheck to a neighbor or acquaintance for them to fulfill their interests. The extent to which individuals are permitted to look after their self-interest in an economy provides another gauge of how free or command-oriented a market is.

Government intervention and regulation in the market constitute another characteristic. In the United States, increasing intervention and regulation has been the trend for the last 50 or 60 years in our economy. I discussed private property and its usage. Government intervention spanning from local governments to state governments and all the way to the federal level, has manifested in various ways. The more government regulations exist, the less free the economy is due to constraints imposed by these regulations. The greater the government interference, limiting free choices, the more it tilts towards a command market. It's not merely about observing what the government desires; it's about scrutinizing different characteristics to discern the choices people are allowed to make concerning resources.

Additionally, we can examine financial systems, competition, price determination, and more. Are financial institutions trustworthy and stable? Generally, the more stable they are, the freer the market tends to be. However, in some command-oriented systems, stability can also exist. Is competition restricted by government or are people allowed to buy and sell as they wish? In other words, are prices determined within a structure that enables individual choices rather than government dictates?

2. Adam Smith, *An Inquiry into the Nature and Causes of the Wealth of Nations* (1776; repr., Indianapolis: Liberty Fund, 1981).

The key factor is where the choices are made in the economy. If choices are allowed to be made in markets by individuals, it signifies a freer market. The more the government intervenes, the more it tilts towards a command market. Several sources can be consulted to precisely gauge how countries are ranked. The Heritage Foundation has a comprehensive ranking[3] indicating that, at present, we do not have a market anywhere near being truly free. Some countries that come close to a free market include Singapore, Taiwan, and New Zealand. New Zealand is particularly interesting; having a son living there, I try to stay updated on developments. Despite being perceived as a socialist country due to recent governmental tendencies, New Zealand still maintains a free market where the aforementioned characteristics are allowed to evolve in a manner that facilitates choices. Distinguishing between a command and free market requires careful consideration. Many free markets tend to lean towards socialist governance. We've witnessed this happen multiple times, only for people to realize it's detrimental to the economy, their livelihood, and their overall well-being. Additionally, some countries venture too far down this path and eventually collapse due to the burden of the command system, as evidenced by Venezuela.

Again, we are discussing a country's economy, not its political or social inclinations. It's crucial to differentiate between these concepts, a distinction that many fail to recognize.

3. The Heritage Foundation, *Index of Economic Freedom 2024* (Washington, DC: The Heritage Foundation, 2024), https://www.heritage.org/index/.

Discussion Questions

1. **The chapter explains that most economies are mixed systems rather than purely free or purely command markets.** Why do you think few countries operate at either extreme, and what might be the benefits and drawbacks of a command market? Free Market? Mixed Market System?
2. **In a free market, profit is described as a return for taking risk rather than something inherently negative.** Do you agree with this view? How does understanding profit as a reward for risk change how you think about businesses and investors?
3. **Adam Smith's idea of self-interest and the "invisible hand" suggests that individuals pursuing their own goals can benefit society as a whole.** Can you think of a real-world example where self-interest leads to positive outcomes for others? Are there situations where it might not?
4. **The chapter uses private property and freedom of choice as indicators of how free a market is.** Based on these characteristics, where do you think the United States falls on the spectrum between a free market and a command market? Explain your reasoning.
5. **Government regulation is presented as a factor that can push an economy toward a command system.** How can government intervention both help and harm an economy? In your opinion, where should the balance be between free markets and regulation?

3 Markets: Supply and Demand

How does the free market actually work? Well, the key lies in the market itself, the place where a buyer and a seller come together to agree on a price and quantity of an item. In this chapter, we will look at both sides of this market, see how they interact, and what causes them to change.

Let's start with the buyer's side of the market, which is called the demand. The demand side of a market shows what people are willing to buy at a given price of a certain item. It is ruled by the law of demand, which states the following: "With everything else held constant, as the price of a product rises, the quantity demanded will fall. As prices fall, the quantity demanded will rise." Of course, you know this already; most people understand that we buy less of a product when the price is high and more of a product when the price is low. The law of demand is just a way to make sure we keep the focus on price and quantity. Holding everything else constant means that anything outside of this market is deemed to have not changed. In other words, we are taking a snapshot and looking at what people are willing to buy at each given price with no other influences.

The seller side of the market is called supply. On the supply side, producers are willing to sell a certain amount of product at each given price. It is ruled by the law of supply, which states the following: 'With everything else held constant, as the price of a product rises, the quantity supplied will rise. As the price falls, the quantity supplied will fall. Again, holding everything else the same, we look at what price does to producers' willingness to sell a product at each given price.

As stated in the beginning, a market is comprised of both the buyer and the seller of a certain product. So, to find out how the market operates, we must put the two sides together. In other words, we must allow supply to meet demand inside the marketplace, holding everything else outside of that market constant. When we do this, we find a point where the decisions of the buyers meet the decisions of the sellers. Another way of saying this is that we have a place where supply and demand intersect. There is a certain price where the amount people are willing to buy is equal to the amount that sellers are willing to sell. In economics, we call this spot equilibrium. It is a point that is said to be efficient; at that point, we produce at the lowest possible cost, and we are allocating the right number of resources into that market so there is no waste and no want.

Any price below this point will lead the market to have a shortage, meaning that more people are demanding the product than there are suppliers of that product. In that case, we see the price of the product being bid up. Just think about eBay when there is an item many people want but a limited supply of that item. At that point, the bid for the item starts rising until it reaches a point where the number of buyers equals the number of sellers. The price will rise until enough people stop demanding it and enough producers begin selling.

This happens in the real world. A few years ago, Hostess had to declare bankruptcy because their costs were too high for their level of revenue. At that point, people started panicking that they would never get to eat another Twinkie. On eBay, there were not many Twinkies being sold; however, there were a lot of people going on eBay to buy Twinkies. Being an economist, I saw a short window of opportunity, and I went to my nearest grocery store and bought 20 boxes of Twinkies. While I was checking out, I put one up on eBay, and by the time I had reached my car, I had sold a box of Twinkies I had bought for $2.50 for $20. When I arrived home, I decided that if I sold all 20 that night, I would go and buy some more tomorrow. By 2 a.m., I had sold all 20 boxes for an average of over $25 a box. The next morning, I was off to the store again, and I purchased 80 more boxes of Twinkies. Over the next few days, I sold a total of 93 boxes of Twinkies for an average price of $20 per box. Again, I had only paid $2.50 per box for each one, so I made a considerable profit.

The economic lesson in this was that there was a market where there was a shortage of the product. As people tried to buy Twinkies on eBay, they continuously bid the price up. Eventually, something changed, and more supply entered eBay, and we saw the price coming down. That is why I sold some boxes at a higher price, and eventually, the price started inching back down. In fact, within a week, the price of Twinkies on eBay went for about $3.00 per box, which is what they sold for in the stores. However, for a short time, there was a chance to make some money as the suppliers moved into the market. Unfortunately for many after those first few days, they were stuck with hundreds and hundreds of boxes of Twinkies, simply because they did not understand economics.

The other side of this is if the price is above equilibrium. In this case, there is more supply of the product than there are actually people willing to buy the product. In this case, the price will drop, pushing the price back down to equilibrium. This can be seen in just about any store when they have too much product on the shelf, and it is not moving. They will drop the price so that more product will sell and continue to do so until the product is gone.

What we see happening here is the invisible hand described by Adam Smith[1], decisions being made in the market to push us to a point of efficiency. Going back to the law of supply and the law of demand, we see that the decisions being made due to price are pushing us to equilibrium. If the price is too high, we see prices drop, which means the quantity supplied will drop and the quantity demanded will go up. This will continue until we reach a point that quantity demanded equals quantity supplied. If the price is too low, then we will see the price starting to go up. As the price rises, the quantity demanded goes down, and the quantity supplied goes up. Again, this will push us to the point of equilibrium. If we are at equilibrium, that means that we have allocated the right number of resources into the market, and no resources were used to make a product that was not wanted, and no one is waiting on resources to be allocated for a product they demand. As far as being productive efficient, to maximize profits, companies will try to cut the cost as much as possible in producing the product, which means that the consumer will get the lowest price possible for the item in a perfectly free market.

1. Adam Smith, *An Inquiry into the Nature and Causes of the Wealth of Nations* (1776; repr., Indianapolis: Liberty Fund, 1981).

Changes in Equilibrium

We have previously assumed that all factors remained constant, observing only a change in price leading to a change in quantity. However, in this section, we will explore the impact of external changes. When factors outside the market change, both the quantity consumers are willing to demand at different prices and the quantity suppliers are willing to sell at different prices are affected.

ON THE DEMAND SIDE:

Consumer preferences significantly influence demand. Preferences, continually evolving, affect how much people are willing to buy of a particular item. For example, the popularity of flip cell phones waned as smartphones emerged, altering demand.

The number of buyers in a market also shapes demand. More buyers increase demand, while fewer buyers decrease it.

Income levels influence demand. Normal goods, such as smartphones, see increased demand with higher incomes. Normal goods are those items we buy more of when our income goes up. In contrast, inferior goods like cheap noodles experience reduced demand as income rises. These inferior goods are usually things we settle for to save money.

Prices of related goods impact demand. Complementary goods, like SUVs and gas, exhibit an inverse relationship in demand. When gas prices rise, SUV sales decrease, and vice versa. Substitute goods, like brand-name versus store-brand products, are affected similarly.

ON THE SUPPLY SIDE:

Cost variations significantly impact supply. Increased costs limit supply, while reduced costs encourage higher production. Technological advancements enhance efficiency, increasing production. Loss of technology decreases efficiency, reducing supply. The number of sellers in a market directly influences supply: more sellers increase supply, while fewer sellers decrease it.

Government intervention also impacts supply. Taxes impose additional expenses on businesses, indirectly affecting consumers who ultimately bear the burden. Subsidies, on the other hand, lower costs, increasing supply.

When factors change on either the supply or demand side, the market experiences new equilibrium, leading to altered equilibrium price and quantity. Demand increases result in higher prices and greater quantities. Conversely, decreased demand leads to lower prices and quantities. On the supply side, increased supply leads to lower prices but higher quantities, while decreased supply raises prices and reduces quantities.

Invisible Hand: Supply and Demand

I have covered a lot in this chapter that really is at the heart of markets and why they work. The decisions being made by buyers and sellers in the marketplace push us to a point of efficiency which is where supply and demand meet. Literally, this is the invisible hand working in everyday life. I believe there is no better mechanism to make sure we are using resources to the best of their ability, though we can see a market fail.

Discussion Questions

1. **The chapter explains that markets reach equilibrium when supply and demand intersect.** Why is equilibrium described as an efficient outcome, and do you think efficiency always leads to fair outcomes for consumers and producers?
2. **The Twinkie example shows how shortages can cause prices to rise quickly.** Do you think it is fair for sellers to raise prices during shortages, or is this simply how markets respond to scarcity? Why or why not?
3. **The law of demand and the law of supply both rely on the idea of "holding everything else constant."** Why is this assumption important when studying markets, and what might happen if many factors change at the same time?
4. **The chapter explains that prices act as signals to both buyers and sellers.** How do rising or falling prices help coordinate decisions in a market, and can you think of a situation where price signals might be confusing or misleading?
5. **Government actions such as taxes and subsidies can change supply and prices.** In your opinion, when might government intervention improve a market outcome, and when might it create new problems?

4 Market Failures

We've spent the first part of the book talking about how effective a free market can be, but there are times when we do witness market failures. This doesn't imply that the price is too high or there's no product on the shelf; it's when one of the sides of the market fails to consider all aspects of that product. Market failures can occur on the demand side as well as on the supply side, and these failures are caused by externalities, factors external to the market that impact it.

A demand-side failure occurs when all of the demand cannot be accounted for inside the market. The easiest example to illustrate this is a fireworks display. When fireworks are displayed after a baseball game on July 4th, people inside the stadium have paid for their tickets and are part of the market. However, people standing outside the stadium, on the street, or even in nearby houses can also view the fireworks without having to pay. They derive some benefit from it, spending time watching the show, but they aren't willing to enter the market to purchase a ticket. This is known as a positive externality, where someone external to the market benefits from what's happening inside the market. Because this demand cannot be captured, the demand numbers are incorrect, leading to a market failure.

On the supply side, failure occurs when the supply doesn't consider all the costs of producing the product. For instance, a company polluting the environment and not factoring in the cost of waste disposal is a case of negative externality. In this scenario, someone external to the market bears the cost. Since supply isn't capturing the full cost, this also constitutes a market failure.

When a market fails, corrective measures are necessary. This provides an opportunity for the government to intervene in the market. While there are instances where government intervention can be beneficial, often, such intervention distorts the market further. We will explore some of these examples later in this chapter.

Public Goods

One area where government intervention is seen is in the case of public goods. Public goods are products or services deemed important for the overall economic health of our community. Although the private market could produce these goods, it might not produce enough. Public education is an example of this. While private schools exist and thrive, relying solely on them would deprive many people of an education. Economists have found that a literate and educated populace fosters better economic growth in the long run. Therefore, we have chosen to let the government supply this public good. Other examples include roadways and libraries.

Many people mistake the presence of public goods as a sign of becoming a socialist nation. However, merely having public goods doesn't make a society socialist. Remember from Chapter 2 that the socialist system is dictated by who owns the resources and who decides how they will be used. A free economy may allow the government to supply some public goods, but that doesn't mean the government does it efficiently. One can easily find waste in the budgets of local school districts. However, the overall trade-off between waste and an educated populace is a positive one.

Government Intervention

Government intervention can sometimes be helpful. As mentioned earlier, most of the time government intervention exacerbates market failures. Let's revisit Chapter 3 and our equilibrium point that led us to efficiency. Many times, governments step in and try to control prices, believing they are helping people when, in fact, it often harms them.

Let's consider a scenario where the government sets a price below equilibrium and prohibits producers from charging more than that price. Since the price is below equilibrium, a shortage occurs. In a normal market, the price would naturally increase. However, since the government has set a price limit, the price remains unchanged, leading to a chronic shortage in the market. Those who manage to obtain the good before it sells out get a good deal. For others, the product is unavailable due to low supply.

Price gouging laws exemplify this phenomenon. While these laws aim to protect consumers from unethical producers, they often result in people going without essential items. The question isn't whether someone is making a high profit; the question is whether the item will be available when people need it. During a natural disaster, essential items sell out quickly. Price gouging laws, which prohibit price increases during emergencies, make the shortage more pronounced. If prices were allowed to rise, people would be willing to bring supplies to the affected area, ensuring availability. Instead, these laws often leave people without necessities.

On the other side, the government can set a price that no one can charge less than for a particular item. If this price is above equilibrium, a surplus is created. In a regular market, the price would fall, moving back towards efficiency. However, if the government mandates a minimum price, a chronic surplus occurs.

The minimum wage is a good example of this scenario. Although it is presented as a means to help low-skilled workers earn a higher wage, it often makes those it aims to help worse off. When the minimum wage increases, more people look for work, increasing the supply of labor. Simultaneously, businesses (the ones who demand labor) look to cut costs. Here, the basic principles of supply and demand intersect. On the supply side (individuals), more people enter the market as the price rises, increasing the quantity supplied of labor. On the demand side (businesses), as price falls, the quantity demanded for labor decreases.

The intention behind the minimum wage is to improve the earnings of low-skilled workers. However, in practice, it often results in these workers losing their jobs. Businesses, facing higher labor costs, cut jobs to maintain profitability. In the long run, prices increase to accommodate these higher wages, meaning that the real earning power of those making minimum wage remains largely unchanged. Moreover, the notion that this only affects low-wage workers is inaccurate. When the minimum wage rises, those earning slightly more than the minimum also expect a raise. Even union members, with contracts that automatically adjust for minimum wage hikes, anticipate increased wages. Consequently, across the economy, labor prices rise, leading to higher prices for goods and services.

These are just a couple of examples illustrating how government intervention often causes more issues than it resolves. Further research would reveal more examples such as rent control, affordable housing initiatives, open space planning, and universal price controls. Often, government attempts to correct market failures result in unintended negative consequences.

Most free-market economists argue that there is a role for government in the economy, at the very least to protect private property rights and uphold contractual law. However, even in these areas, government intervention requires careful consideration. It's important to understand that while some situations may feel unfair, it doesn't necessarily mean there's a market failure. Keynesian economics argues that markets cannot function without government intervention, but this statement has been stretched too far in practice.

Discussion Questions

1. **How do positive and negative externalities lead to market failures, and why do they cause prices or quantities to be inaccurate?** Use examples such as fireworks displays or environmental pollution to support your answer.
2. **Why might the private market underproduce public goods like education, roads, or libraries?** Do you agree that government involvement is justified in these cases? Why or why not?
3. **In what ways can government intervention attempt to fix market failures, and why might these interventions sometimes make the situation worse?** Refer to price controls or regulations discussed in the chapter.
4. **How do price ceilings, such as price gouging laws, affect supply and demand during emergencies?** Do you think availability or affordability is more important in these situations? Explain your reasoning.
5. **What are the intended goals of the minimum wage, and what unintended consequences might result from it according to supply and demand theory?** Do you think these trade-offs are worth it? Why or why not?

5 Introduction to the Macroeconomy

After covering basic economics, it's time to delve into the two primary branches: Macroeconomic and Microeconomic. Microeconomics deals with the study of individuals within the economy, encompassing people, households, businesses, and markets for individual products. While Microeconomic principles are generally agreed upon in economics, disagreements arise when applying these principles to the overall economy.

Macroeconomics examines the entire economic landscape and encompasses various schools of thought, such as Classical, Keynesian, Neo-classical, Austrian, Monetarist, and the Chicago School of Economics. I won't delve into detailed definitions here, as even within these schools, debates persist about how these principles interact. My objective is not to favor one over the other but to provide you with a practical understanding of our current economic functioning. It's noteworthy that the United States government primarily operates with a Keynesian economic framework.

Our exploration begins with defining terms to analyze the overall economy. We'll introduce the business cycle, which encapsulates the economy's peaks and troughs, along with the indicators used to identify these cycles. We'll also touch on macroeconomic theories about how the overall economy functions and conclude the Macroeconomic section with government interventions: fiscal policy and monetary policy. To comprehend monetary policy, we first need to understand the banking system, primarily focusing on the United States, which we will discuss in a dedicated chapter.

Business Cycle

The economy experiences cycles of expansion and contraction known as the business cycle, comprised of four phases: peak, recession, trough, and expansion. Identifying these phases involves observing indicators that reflect where we stand in the cycle. These indicators, discussed in this chapter, include major indicators like real GDP, unemployment, and inflation.

Gross Domestic Product (GDP)

Our first indicator is GDP, used to evaluate an economy's output during a specific period. Quantity cannot be used since one hamburger and one automobile would not make sense being counted just as two items, as well as not being able to put a true number to services. Therefore, we use the total price of final goods and services sold. This is why GDP appears in dollars. Calculating GDP involves summing up consumer spending, gross business investment in capital(assets), government spending on goods and services, and net exports (exports-imports). Final products are used because the final price will include all other products that were purchased to produce it. This means we ignore what are called intermediate goods, which are components used in the final product. Those sales are excluded because it would lead to double counts. It is good to note that we do not count any financial transactions, such as money transfers and bond purchases. These do not have any production behind them, so it is not output. Secondhand sales are also excluded since they would have been counted as a final product in the year they were produced.

GDP is measured in nominal terms, indicating its value without adjusting for price changes(inflation). To assess the economy over time, we need to adjust the figure based on what has happened with the value of the dollar. Nominal GDP is converted into real GDP, where nominal is the original unadjusted total and real adjusts for price changes using a price index. A price index indexes price to one year, called a base year. Essentially what we are doing is converting all the dollars across a time period into one year's dollars.

The price index can be looked at as a basket of goods and services that we would collect prices on every year. The prices are then compared over the years to see the changes. A base year is then picked, and the other years are indexed to that year. Think of it as using the same ruler for each year.

Real GDP then can be used to analyze output trends across the business cycle phases. It is not a perfect tool, but if collected the same way every year, it can be used to judge the increase or decrease in production over time. This is why it is said to be an indicator of where we are in the cycle.

Unemployment

Unemployment gauges the percentage of people actively seeking employment within the labor force. The labor force is comprised of those over 16 years of age that are employed and those actively looking for jobs. People must be actively looking for a job to allow us to track them, it does not include discouraged workers which are people who have given up seeking employment. This measure also does not measure part-time employees seeking full-time work and individuals working below their skill levels. They would be considered employed even though they are underemployed. Discouraged workers have joined others that are "not in the labor force". This would also include anyone who is not looking for a job, such as stay home parents, retirees, students, patients and those in the penal system.

Unemployment can be further categorized into frictional, structural, and cyclical unemployment. Frictional includes people who are moving between jobs, meaning they will only be unemployed for a short time. Structural counts those people that have lost a job because their skills are no longer needed in an industry or location. Frictional and structural unemployment are always present, constituting what economists call the natural rate of unemployment. Cyclical unemployment fluctuates with the business cycle, indicating economic health. If we have this type happening, it indicates we are in a recession. So, economist spend the most time tracking this type.

Inflation

The last indicator we will look at is inflation. Inflation signifies a general rise in the price level in an economy. It measures the decrease in the value of money over time. This used to be one of the most boring chapters in my class, until 2022. It was hard to describe it to students who had never experienced it. After the increase of inflation, it quickly became one of the most interesting sections and prompted much discussion.

For those that want to explore inflation deeper, take a look at core inflation. The CPI (Consumer Price Index) is used to track inflation in the US, it includes energy and food prices. These two groups vary drastically during the year causing issues with tracking the rate. Gas prices in the summer, fuel oil in the winter, harvest times across the country, all can distort the overall rate. Therefore, we look at core inflation where these two categories are pulled out and that gives us a more stable look at prices.

Two causes of inflation exist: one on the supply side which is called cost-push and one on the demand called demand-pull inflation. Cost-push inflation originates from increased production costs, while demand-pull inflation arises from excess money in the economy chasing limited goods, leading to rising prices. These inflation types impact different economic sectors during various phases of the business cycle, potentially causing stagflation – a scenario with rising prices, high unemployment, and economic decline. During COIVD and after, we experienced both types as we saw record levels in the inflation rate.

One last type to look at is hyperinflation. This happens in a country when we see confidence lost in the currency. It happened in Post-War World I Germany where the inflation rate hit 21% per day and helped Hitler come to power. It also hit Zimbabwe in 2007 with a 98% daily increase in prices and most recently in Venezuela where the rate topped at only 4% per day leading to 221% month over month in 2016. This is small compared to the first two, however once you hit over 1% per day, the economy is experiencing hyperinflation.[1]

---

1. Hanke, Steve H., "Venezuela Enters the Record Book, Officially Hyperinflates," *Cato at Liberty* (blog), December 12, 2016, Cato Institute, https://www.cato.org/blog/venezuela-enters-record-book-officially-hyperinflates (accessed January 15, 2026).

Conclusion

While this chapter focuses on three major indicators, it's crucial to acknowledge the complexity of analyzing the economy. Numerous indicators exist, causing considerable debate and analysis. Economic conditions constantly change, making it challenging to interpret indicators definitively. The macroeconomy remains a subject of extensive discussion among economists. While micro fundamentals are widely agreed upon, their translation to the macroeconomy results in diverse applications and interpretations, underscoring the complexity of understanding our economic landscape. Analyzing these indicators provides a directional sense of economic trends, helping anticipate future developments.

Discussion Questions

1. **Microeconomics and macroeconomics often use the same basic ideas, yet economists disagree more at the macro level.** Why do you think it is harder to agree on how the overall economy works compared to individual markets or businesses?
2. **The business cycle moves through expansion, peak, recession, and trough.** How does each of the three major indicators discussed (GDP, unemployment, or inflation) access the cycle?
3. **Real GDP adjusts nominal GDP for inflation using a price index.** Why is it important to make this adjustment when comparing economic output over time, and what problems might arise if we only looked at nominal GDP?
4. **Unemployment statistics do not include discouraged workers or underemployed individuals.** How might this affect the way we interpret the health of the labor market, especially during a recession?
5. **Inflation can be caused by both cost-push and demand-pull forces.** Based on recent economic events discussed in the chapter, how can having both types of inflation at the same time make economic policy more difficult?

6 Macro Theory

While this is a preliminary exploration of economics, it's essential to introduce you to an overarching model for the macroeconomy. I'll outline some fundamental structures of the overall economy and illustrate how they interact in one of the simplest models used in the overview. First, we'll examine how people spend and save their money and understand how it impacts the entire economy. Then, we'll delve into something called the multiplier effect, showing how money circulates and how many times it is spent within a given time frame. Finally, we'll integrate these concepts using a model similar to Chapter 3, examining the overall supply and demand within an economy. Let's begin.

Consumption and Savings

All societies exhibit a natural tendency (or propensity) to consume and save money. Based on these preferences, we can observe how the saving and spending of money affects the overall economy. I'll introduce a couple of economic terms to help understand the effects of this consumption and saving.

The Marginal Propensity to Consume (MPC) and Marginal Propensity to Save (MPS) are two ratios that allow us to model the money flow in society. People who receive extra income tend to save some and spend some. The more they spend, the more it influences the overall consumption within our model. For instance, if you receive an additional $100 in your paycheck, how much of it will you spend, and how much will you save? The more you spend, the more the economy grows. If you spend $80 of that extra $100, that $80 becomes new income for someone else. They then spend $64 and save $18. The $64 spent becomes new income, and so on and so on. As this process continues, the initial $100 turns into several hundred dollars of new income for various individuals.

In this simple model, the MPC and MPS show us how much extra income will be spent and how much will be saved. Understanding these numbers helps us comprehend how new income multiplies through the economy. This is crucial because there are four components to spending in the economy (refer to real GDP).

It is wise to point out, that there are many other opinions about consumption and savings. Many feel like the savings side is more important than consumption, since it makes funds available for investment. Suffice it to say that I could write another book on just the opinions on this topic from the different schools of economic thoughts.

Multiplier Effect

The described phenomenon from the section above is known as the multiplier effect, which can be observed across various expenditures in an economy. When someone consumes, it becomes income for someone else, initiating the multiplier effect. This also occurs when businesses make investments, the government spends money, or there is a change in net exports. Each time one of these GDP components changes, it not only impacts the initial spending but also has a multiplier effect based on how much of their new income people. The higher the multiplier, the faster the economy grows, although inflation is a concern.

Conversely, when someone decides not to spend money, it results in lost income for someone else in the economy. As expenditures contract, the multiplier effect intensifies this contraction. So, when a reduction in spending occurs, not only does the initial slowdown happen, but it multiplies throughout the economy. This is what can deepen a recession, like we saw in 2008.

Overall Economic Model

Let's integrate all these concepts using a model similar to the one in Chapter 3 - Supply & Demand. Here, we modify our main model's demand, considering not just one product but the demand for all goods and services in our system. Similarly, on the supply side, we evaluate the supply of all goods and services in the economy. To depict this accurately, we consider the price level instead of individual prices and the dollar value of all final goods and services. This aligns with what we've learned in earlier chapters: inflation represents a general rise in the price level, guiding us to assess our overall prices.

At this point, demand is termed aggregate demand, aggregating everything together. It indicates the amount of final output consumers want at each given price level. It's influenced by four factors: consumption, business investment, government spending, and net exports. These are familiar from the expenditure approach of GDP. These four elements determine the overall demand in the economy.

On the supply side, we have aggregate supply, signifying the total products to be put into the economy at each given price level. Factors that affect this include resource cost, technology, and government intervention, all involving the cost of business for producers.

Now, let's explore what happens when aggregate demand changes. If there's an increase in consumption by households, it leads to an initial change in overall product demand. However, as people buy more products this triggers the multiplier effect. Thus, demand not only changes due to the initial consumption change but also multiplies due to the effect we discussed earlier. This holds true for all four GDP components. If business investment or government spending increases, it sets off the multiplier effect in addition to the initial change in expenditures. Considering what you've learned about demand, as demand increases, prices go up, leading to a rise in the price level. If this continues, it leads to demand-pull inflation. The reverse happens if business investment decreases; people lose income, reducing expenditures, and triggering the multiplier effect. If this continues, it can lead to a recession.

On the supply side, if costs increase, the quantity of products that can be produced decreases, causing a supply contraction, potentially leading to cost-push inflation. Conversely, if costs decrease, production increases, fostering long-term economic growth.

What has been described in this chapter is a fundamental overview of the macroeconomy. There are extensive discussions and debates on how these elements work together, leading to the various schools of thought mentioned earlier in this book. These debates will likely continue for years to come. Regardless of the school of thought analyzing the situation, they will have to start with a basic model.

Discussion Questions

1. How do the marginal propensity to consume (MPC) and marginal propensity to save (MPS) help explain why a small increase in income can lead to a much larger increase in total economic activity?
2. Using the multiplier effect, explain how one person's spending becomes another person's income. Why can this process strengthen both economic growth and economic downturns?
3. Why do some economists argue that saving is just as important as spending for the health of an economy? How does this viewpoint differ from the focus on consumption in the multiplier effect?
4. What are the four components of aggregate demand, and how can a change in just one of them affect the entire economy? Provide a real-world example.
5. **Compare demand-pull inflation and cost-push inflation.** How do changes in aggregate demand and aggregate supply lead to these two different types of inflation?

7 Fiscal Policy and The National Debt

Having explored the overall economy through the business cycle and a basic model, let's take a look into how the government intervenes in this process. The first method we will examine is fiscal policy, which refers to deliberate changes in taxing and spending by the government aimed at influencing the economy. We are not just talking about general spending and taxing, but about attempts to impact the business cycle through these policies. We will explore what the government believes it should do during times of recession and inflation, as well as the measures they consider to promote economic growth.

During a recession, the government often implements policies to stimulate economic growth and pull the economy out of the downturn. This is typically done by either cutting taxes or increasing government spending. Using our GDP formula, it's clear that government spending directly influences GDP. An increase in government spending not only directly boosts GDP but also triggers the multiplier effect, as people receive new income and spend it based on their marginal propensity to consume.

Taxation is a bit more complex to grasp, but it becomes clearer upon closer examination. Taxes affect households and businesses, but let's focus on households for now. The amount of money someone takes home in their paycheck is their disposable income, as it is the portion of the check they can use as they wish. Gross income, the total compensation for work, is taxed by the government before it reaches the individual (the Roman Empire would be impressed). Therefore, changes in tax rates directly impact disposable income. If the government reduces tax rates, people have more disposable income, leading to increased consumption and savings. This increased consumption becomes new income for others, initiating the multiplier effect. Tax cuts can also be achieved through methods such as tax rebates, which inject money directly into consumers' hands, stimulating spending and multiplying through the economy.

On the flip side, during an economic expansion that leads to inflation, the government may decide to implement measures to counter it. These could include reducing government spending, which would decrease GDP not only initially but also through the multiplier effect. Slowing down growth helps pull down the price level as economic activity diminishes. Alternatively, the government can raise taxes, reducing disposable income and thereby decreasing consumption. This reduction in consumption affects others' income, leading to a decrease in GDP.

The choice of policy tools depends largely on one's perspective on the role of government. Those in favor of a larger government might advocate for increased government spending during a recession, giving more market power to the government. In times of inflation, raising taxes provides the government with more funds to spend, augmenting its influence. Conversely, proponents of smaller government might advocate for tax cuts during a recession, putting more money directly into consumers' pockets to stimulate the economy. During inflationary periods, cutting government spending diminishes government power. This straightforward analysis illuminates the stance on big government versus small government within the realm of governance.

While some schools of thought consider fiscal policy a necessary mandate, others view it as perilous. The ongoing debate stems from the inherent challenge: economics lacks the controlled laboratory setting that other disciplines enjoy. In the final chapter, I will share my perspective on this process.

National Debt

A discussion of Fiscal Policy in the US naturally leads us to discuss deficits and surplus. Summing these from the beginning of the country gives us the national debt which at the time of this book is over $38 trillion dollars. We will get to this but first let's start with how we got here.

Governments are supposed to have a budget, hopefully balanced (a dream in the US). If they go into a year balanced and inflation rears its head, they will use contractionary fiscal policy, raise taxes or cut spending. Either of these will lead to the government not spending all the budget causing a surplus. If a recession happens, they will use expansionary fiscal policy leading to a decrease in taxes or an increase in government spending, causing a deficit. If there are more deficits than surpluses it leads to having to borrow money.

Governments usually borrow money by selling bonds and this is the case for the United States. The debt that is talked about is outstanding US securities which I believe is completely out of control, growing from $4 trillion to $38+ trillion in 25 years. Now, this has not all been caused by fiscal policy, but big chunks were added in 2008 and during the COVID pandemic as the government tried to stimulate the economy during a recession.

Have you ever thought about how big 1 trillion is in practice? Let's look at a trillion seconds, how long ago in history would that take us? Fall of the Berlin wall? WWII? Civil War? Revolutionary war? Middle Ages? No, further back. Roman Empire? Pharaohs in Egypt? It was about 32,000 years ago. With this in mind, look again at the debt. We are not 1 trillion in debt as a country, but $38+ trillion. Some believe it is not a big deal, but this is real money. People are holding this as investment for retirement, in pension funds and other investment instruments. If it is not paid back, it would collapse our economy.

We will address this again in the last chapter, we must get this under control. Some, including me, believe that this is the biggest issue facing the US.

Discussion Questions

1. What is fiscal policy, and how does the government use changes in taxes and spending differently during a recession versus during inflation?
2. How do tax cuts increase disposable income, and why can this lead to a multiplier effect in the economy?
3. Why might people who support a larger role for government prefer increased government spending during a recession, while those who favor smaller government prefer tax cuts?
4. What is the difference between a budget deficit and a budget surplus, and how do repeated deficits contribute to the national debt?
5. Why might a large national debt be viewed as a serious economic problem, even though government debt is often held as investments like bonds and retirement funds?

8 What is Money?

We have been concentrating on the basic definition of economics; the study of choices being made in scarcity with resources. As you have noticed in the book, we have talked a lot about money, so let's spend a little time defining money.

Money allows us to easily turn resources into the items we desire. Instead of having to barter for what we want, or in other words, trade what we have for something someone else has, we can just use some form of payment to sell our resources and then buy the items we want to consume. This means money can really be anything that people accept as a medium of exchange, which is one of the fundamental properties of money. It is used in an economy to buy and sell products and resources. Money has to be able to be used as a store of value. It should be able to be held over time and still have worth. Money also should be a unit of account used in the classification of the value of products, resources, and accounts, such as a checking or retirement account. If an item fits these three definitions, it is considered money. Today, we think of it as some form of currency and coins that we use to exchange, but throughout history, it has taken many forms, including shells, seeds, and stones. As long as people in the economy associate value with it and it meets these three definitions, we will consider it money.

The next thing we want to look at is how quickly you can take that money and turn it into a form that you can buy something at a point of sale. While cash in your pocket is considered money, so are your 401(k) and your savings accounts. They all take a different amount of time to be turned into money that you can actually spend. This is known as liquidity, and it is what central banks base the money supply of a country on. In the United States, we will see that the Federal Reserve system is our central bank, and they determine what is part of the M1, M2, and other money supplies. As you move up, each increment of money supply includes the money supply below it, so M2 includes M1 plus near monies. Recently in the United States, the actual definitions have been altered. Suffice it to say that they all are built on liquidity. The M1 in the United States is the most liquid form of money and includes our currency, coins, and checkable deposits. Checkable deposits are those funds in a checking account that a check can be written on, or a debit card can be swiped at a point of sale.

A money supply can be backed by many different things, and in the past, we have seen it based many times on precious metals such as gold and silver. It can be built on anything of value, but it can also be made without backing. This is called fiat money, and it means that the only thing really backing the currency is someone's guarantee of its value. That is the case in the United States, we take the government's word that the money is legal tender and therefore is worth something. The US Dollar was backed by gold up until the 1930s, and loosely by gold until the 1970s, but after that there is nothing physical that backs it. It is still the only currency used on the petroleum market, which does give it some worth backing. Another reason you might say money has value is that it is usually being held as debt, so people want it to remain worth something. In general, most people have faith that the paper in your pocket has some type of value.

Fractional Reserve System

This brings us to how money is created in different systems. You can have systems that are fully backed with the money in the bank, but that is unusual in this day and time. Most countries have some type of fractional reserve system. This simply means that the bank is only keeping a fraction of the deposits that have been entrusted to them, while they loan out everything above that amount.

This system has come about from many different origins, but the one considered to be the most important to look at is the goldsmiths from the Middle Ages. Goldsmiths, like other artisans, dealt with fine metal and were usually the ones who would hold deposits of gold for the customers. They would issue receipts for those deposits; when someone wanted to use the gold, they would come to redeem it and go purchase the item they were looking to buy. Then the vendor would usually bring the gold back to the goldsmith for storage, and a new receipt would be issued. Over time, people began to get weary of going and getting gold to buy something, so they began just endorsing the receipts over to the vendor they were purchasing from. This became one of the earliest forms of paper money as people used the receipts as we use our money today. The goldsmiths then realized the gold was not moving and came up with the idea to issue new receipts on the same gold and loan those receipts out. They would charge interest from the borrowers; then would pay interest on their depositors' gold, and a new form of banking was born. At any given time, there was only a fraction of gold with a goldsmith to cover all the receipts that were in circulation.

Fast forward to today, and we see the same scenario playing out. All banks only keep a fraction of the cash on hand for their deposits, and they lend out the other money. In the US, there is currently no reserve amount required, so a bank can loan out all the money on deposit. This does not happen because the bank must remain solvent each day, i.e. cover their liabilities. The biggest issue with this type of system is the fear of bank runs where everyone wants to pull their deposits at once; this can collapse a banking system. There are safeguards in place to ensure this does not happen, but there is never a full guarantee. This type of system allows the growth of an economy in a greater way than other systems.

United States Monetary System

Let's take a closer look at this in the United States. The Federal Reserve governs how much of depositors' money banks are required to keep on hand (again, this is set at zero currently). This is called required reserves. A bank can only lend out those reserves above required reserves, called excess reserves. When a bank loans out its excess reserves, it is literally creating money because it is loaning out someone else's money so two different people have a right to that money.

If someone puts $1000 in their checking account, and let's say that the reserve requirement set by the Fed is 10%, that means the bank must keep $100 for its required reserves and it will have excess reserves of $900. They can loan out up to $900 from that first deposit. The next step is that the $900 is loaned; usually, someone will deposit it into the bank, and that makes it another deposit, and then the bank will keep $90 in required reserves and lend out $810. The cycle continues in that manner, which means that initial $1000 deposit ends up creating much more money in the system through the lending process. Lending creates money in this process, so therefore, paying off loans destroys money. Again, staying away from a lot of math, there is something called a simple money multiplier. It can estimate what that initial thousand dollars will do in the system. The simple money multiplier is simply dividing the reserve requirement into one, giving us a number that we can multiply to determine the potential money created in the system from one deposit. The money multiplier tells us how much one dollar of excess reserves can potentially create in the system. The actual multiplier is much more complicated, but this simple one allows us to see the potential in lending. In our example, the initial $1000 deposit leads to a total of $10,000 in the system.

Federal Reserve System

We have mentioned the Federal Reserve system, the Fed, in this chapter several times. Let's take a closer look at this structure inside the United States. As mentioned, it acts as a central bank the same way in other countries they have a central bank. The central bank is in charge of controlling the money supply in the country. Our system is made up of a board of governors, a federal open market committee, and 12 regional banks. The public does not do business with these banks; only commercial banks do business with the federal reserve. Think of it as the banker's bank. Banks have their reserves deposited with their regional Federal Reserve Bank and it is used to clear checks and other ACH (like debit card swipes) payments inside the system. Other jobs of the federal reserve is to supervise banks, issue currency, (they do not print the money, they just issue it for the US treasury), act as the fiscal agent for the US government, the lender of last resort for banks (a mechanism for banks to cover their liabilities at the end of the day if they are short), and control the money supply.

The most important job however is controlling the money supply. They decide how much potential money is in the system at any given time by affecting excess reserves. We will discuss this in more detail in the next chapter as well as look at monetary policy.

Discussion Questions

1. What are the three main functions of money, and why must something meet all three to be considered money? Can you think of an example that might meet some functions but not all?
2. Why did societies move from barter systems to using money, and how does money make economic exchange easier and more efficient?
3. What is liquidity, and why are some forms of money, like cash or checking accounts, considered more liquid than 401K accounts or retirement accounts?
4. How does a fractional reserve banking system allow banks to create money, and why can this system help an economy grow?
5. What role does the Federal Reserve play in the U.S. monetary system, and why is controlling the money supply considered its most important responsibility?

9 Monetary Policy

Monetary policy involves manipulating the money supply to impact the overall economy. Reflecting on the components of GDP (consumption, investment, government spending, and net exports), we can observe how changes in interest rates influence spending within the economy. To comprehend this process, we'll start by examining the market for money, focusing on its supply and demand.

The price paid to use money is known as interest. Although there are various interest rates based on different factors, the federal funds rate serves as a foundational benchmark, influencing all other rates. The federal funds market, where banks lend money to one another to cover daily liabilities, is pivotal. The Federal Reserve aims to target this rate by adjusting the money supply, thereby manipulating the federal funds rate in the market.

The market for money operates like other markets we have explored, with both a supply side and a demand side. On the demand side, the amount of money needed for purchasing goods and services (GDP) and assets is essential. There is always an amount of output that will be needed to satisfy the public no matter what the interest rate is at the time. This is usually referred to as the transaction demand for money. Basically, we are going to buy a certain amount of food, gas, clothing, etc. no matter if the rate is high or low. Therefore, this demand is not affected by the interest rate.

When businesses seek to expand their capital or households look to consume past the point mentioned above, the interest rate affects their demand. Therefore, the interest rate and the demand for money for assets are inversely related. For instance, when interest rates are low, businesses invest more and consumers buy more, stimulating economic growth. By combining the demand for GDP and assets, we arrive at the total demand for money, forming one side of the market.

On the supply side, the Federal Reserve controls the money supply in the United States. By adjusting this supply, the Federal Reserve can influence the equilibrium in the market, thus changing the interest rate. The interest rate acts as the price of using someone else's money, with quantity representing the dollars being demanded and supplied. Increasing the money supply means there's more money available, making it cheaper, thereby reducing the interest rate. Conversely, contracting the money supply increases its value, making it more expensive, thus raising the interest rate.

Manipulating the money supply involves changing the excess reserves in the system, accomplished through various monetary policy tools. These tools encompass the reserve requirement, discount rate, interest on reserves, auction facilities, and open market operations. The reserve requirement directly influences excess reserves by specifying the percentage of deposits that banks must hold. The discount rate represents the rate at which the Fed lends money to banks overnight, impacting the federal funds rate. Interest on reserves refers to the interest paid by the Fed to banks on their deposits, affecting lending activities. Auction facilities are long-term loans to banks.

The primary tool employed by the Fed is open market operations. The Federal Open Market Committee (FOMC) helps determine the target interest rate and how to achieve it. Open market operations involve buying and selling bonds on the open market, usually U.S. government debt. By purchasing bonds, the Fed injects money into the system, lowering interest rates. They offer to buy bonds from the public, the money for payment then ends up in a banking account and the process of lending begins. Selling bonds absorbs money, increasing interest rates. Money leaves the public bank accounts forcing the money supply to contract.

However, implementing monetary policy poses challenges. There's a recognition lag due to the time it takes to identify economic trends. An administrative lag exists as it takes time to adjust the money supply. Additionally, a liquidity trap can occur where injected money isn't lent out, hindering its impact. Lastly, the business cycle's complexity necessitates educated estimations in policy decisions.

Discussion Questions

1. What is monetary policy, and how does changing the money supply affect interest rates and spending in the economy?
2. Why is the federal funds rate considered the key interest rate in the U.S. economy, and how does it influence other interest rates?
3. What is the difference between transaction demand for money and demand for money as an asset, and why does interest rate only affect one of them?
4. How do open market operations work, and why are they the Federal Reserve's primary tool for influencing the money supply?
5. What challenges or limitations make monetary policy difficult to carry out effectively, such as time lags or a liquidity trap?

10 Consumer Actions

You now have read how the overall economy functions, so let's go back to the individual level. In this chapter, we will explore one of the primary topics in microeconomics: consumer behavior. As mentioned earlier in the book, microeconomics delves into the actions of individuals in the economy, encompassing people, businesses, and markets. Over the next few chapters, we will explore several topics forming the foundation of economics. In this chapter, our focus lies in understanding how individuals make decisions regarding the use of their resources. It's important to note that this area of study comprises numerous theories, and we will just cover a couple in this chapter to establish a foundational understanding of consumer behavior.

First, let's examine the reason behind our consumption of goods and services. We engage in consumption because these goods and services bring us contentment; economists refer to this contentment as utility. Utility represents the satisfaction or pleasure derived from consuming a product. The underlying assumption is that most individuals aim to maximize utility using their limited resources. To comprehend this, we initially consider total utility, which signifies the satisfaction derived from consuming the same product at various quantities. However, a more critical aspect to analyze is known as marginal utility, denoting the extra satisfaction gained from consuming one more unit of a product. For instance, with pizza, the first slice provides significant satisfaction, but as consumption continues, each subsequent slice offers diminishing satisfaction. This diminishing return on utility is a universal experience, albeit varying for different individuals. Utility, though essential, is challenging to quantify and apply universally. Furthermore, excessive consumption can lead to negative utility. Overeating during occasions like Thanksgiving can result in discomfort, causing a reduction in overall satisfaction, demonstrating the concept of negative utility.

Consumer behavior theories assume rational decision-making, although economists acknowledge that not everyone acts rationally all the time. While occasional irrational purchases occur, individuals tend to spend their money rationally, considering the utility derived from products and their prices. It's worth noting that businesses constantly attempt to influence irrational purchases, often using impulse-buying tactics at checkout counters, advertising, and pressure tactics.

One theory says that consumers will continue buying products based on the utility received and the price, ensuring that the utility per dollar spent on each item remains relatively equal. This theory emphasizes a correlation between the utility and the cost of items purchased.

Another theory incorporates a combination of products aligned with a budget constraint, as discussed earlier. This theory asserts that individuals are indifferent to specific combinations of goods and services and the budget constraint will determine the combination they will consume. As income increases, the quantity of items purchasable also grows. This theory accounts for price changes, altering the combinations to which consumers remain indifferent.

Without delving into intricate graphs, the key takeaway is that people generally utilize their resources rationally. Most individuals do not squander their income, at least not for extended periods. While exceptions exist due to societal preferences and evolving norms, rational consumption remains a prevalent behavior.

These have been the theories that have prevailed for many decades, but I would be remiss if I did not mention that over the last several decades there is a school of thought that would say that all decisions are irrational. While some of their arguments are interesting, I do not see where they hold in the long run for most of the population. It is very easy to cherry pick situations and data that can support any hypothesis, just like in any discipline. Adam Smith's assertions in his book still hold, people will look after their self-interests and being irrational does not help them. One last thought, what may look irrational to an outside observer may be rational to the person in the situation.

Discussion Questions

1. What is utility, and how does the idea of marginal utility help explain why people do not consume unlimited amounts of the same good, such as pizza or dessert?
2. Can you think of a time when consuming more of something led to negative utility for you?
3. **Economists often assume that consumers act rationally.** Do you agree with this assumption overall? Why or why not, and how do impulse buying and advertising challenge this idea?
4. Explain the theory that consumers try to keep the utility per dollar spent equal across products. How might this theory influence how a student decides to spend money on food, entertainment, or textbooks?
5. **The chapter suggests that what looks irrational to an outsider may be rational to the individual.** Can you give an example of a purchase that might seem irrational to others but makes sense given a person's preferences or situation?

11 Production Cost

In this chapter, we investigate the considerations businesses make when deciding what to supply in the market. Economics employs unique concepts, that diverge from traditional accounting terms by incorporating opportunity costs alongside explicit costs. Explicit costs are payments made for items, while implicit costs encompass the opportunity costs of using self-owned resources and normal profits, reflecting the assumed profit businesses aim to make.

Opportunity costs of utilizing self-owned resources are often overlooked. For instance, a landscape company employing an already-owned truck fails to account for its replacement cost. Implicit costs need inclusion in business evaluations, that is to say any self-owned resources need to be accounted for since they could be used somewhere else to generate income. Normal profits are also integrated, representing the anticipated profit in the industry. There would be no reason to have a business without a normal return on investment. This means a return that could be made somewhere else on the market. Any surplus above these implicit costs, added to explicit or accounting cost constitutes economic profit. This economic profit makes the industry attractive to entrepreneurs who see a chance for a high return. If the market is free, we would see entry into the industry, which would drive down the price (remember from our supply model) and over time eliminate the economic profit leaving only a normal profit.

Production inputs are categorized into fixed and variable inputs, outlined by short-run and long-run periods. Fixed inputs are unalterable in the short run, examples being capital goods like trucks or business spaces. Variable inputs, on the other hand, fluctuate with production levels and directly contribute to output, such as copy paper for a copy shop or wood for a cabinet maker.

These inputs translate to fixed and variable costs. Fixed costs, like rent or equipment payments, persist regardless of production, while variable costs increase with higher production and decrease with lower production. Analyzing fixed and variable costs enables businesses to decide on production levels and whether to continue production.

Time periods are divided into short run and long run based on cost variability. The short run encompasses fixed costs and variable costs, while the long run involves only variable costs. All decisions can be made about production in the long run. However, any commitment to contracts or payments reverts the business back to the short run, necessitating detailed analysis. This means businesses live in the short run, so we spend most of our time analyzing that period.

In analyzing production, total product, average product, and marginal product are crucial metrics. Total product denotes a company's overall output with a set of fixed inputs, adding the variable ones. Average product looks at the average output based on an input. Marginal product signifies the extra output resulting from an additional unit of input. There is a point of diminishing returns where adding more variable inputs to fixed inputs results in decreased productivity, mirroring the concept of negative utility. This can be seen in a company that has too many employees for the number of machines they have in the production process. Think of a copy shop with two copy machines. One employee could run them both, but a second employee would help keep production up. You could even make the case that a third employee could increase output by taking orders and bringing the supplies to the operators. We may see an increase in output as we add variable inputs(workers) to fixed inputs(copiers), but at some point, adding more workers will end up decreasing the output per input. Continuing to add them would end up pulling total production down. Why? People would be standing around, getting in each other's way or maybe talking too much. The key is to find the right mix.

In the short run, fixed costs and variable costs combined result in total cost. Average cost per unit can be derived by dividing fixed cost, variable cost, and total cost by production quantity. This gives you average fixed cost, average variable cost and average total cost. Comparing average cost to the selling price indicates economic profit, normal profit, economic loss, or shutdown points. If the price surpasses average total cost, economic profit is made. If equal, normal profit is attained. If below, a decision between continuing at a loss or shutting down must be made, considering fixed costs. If you can cover your fixed costs in the short run and some variable, you would operate at a loss until the long run when adjustments could be made.

Long-run adjustments involve renegotiating contracts, changing production materials, or finding more cost-effective methods. Adjustments aim for economies of scale, achieving optimal efficiency and lowest possible costs. This culminates in constant returns to scale. However, exceeding this point results in diseconomies of scale, where costs increase due to inefficiencies. Marginal cost and marginal revenue analysis is pivotal for profit maximization, aligning production quantity and price to consumer demand. As in previous discussions, marginal means extra. Marginal revenue is the extra amount you will get for selling one more piece of product and Marginal cost is the extra cost for producing it. Marginal cost becomes the supply curve, indicating the amount producers are willing to supply at each price level.

In the next chapter, these concepts will be utilized to identify the profit-maximizing point in production, demonstrating that only one industry achieves this point, while others fall below it.

Discussion Questions

1. What is the difference between explicit costs and implicit costs, and why is it important for businesses to consider opportunity costs when making production decisions?
2. How do fixed inputs and variable inputs differ in the short run, and how does this difference affect a firm's fixed and variable costs? Can you give a real-world example?
3. Explain the concept of diminishing returns. Why does adding more workers or materials eventually lead to smaller increases in output when some inputs are fixed?
4. How do average total cost and price help a business decide whether it is making an economic profit, normal profit, or an economic loss? Why might a firm continue to operate even when it is losing money in the short run?

12 Industry/Market Structures

In this chapter, we explore the diverse structures of markets and industries, including purely competitive markets, monopolistic competition markets, oligopolies, and monopolies. Each type has distinct characteristics, efficiencies, and real-world applications. Additionally, we analyze how the cost concepts discussed in the previous chapter influence production decisions in these industries.

Purely Competitive Market

A purely competitive market features numerous sellers, none of whom have control over prices. The product is the exact same across all businesses which ensures no company has any power to influence the market. Competition ensures that prices are driven down to the lowest possible point. In theory, this market reaches equilibrium, achieving both the productive and allocative efficiency that we spoke of in an earlier chapter.

In reality, purely competitive markets are rare if nonexistent. Agricultural markets come close but don't fully meet the criteria due to the absence of absolute homogeneity in products. In these markets, marginal revenue equals price, and marginal cost equals supply, representing the equilibrium point. Maximum profit for a company will happen where marginal cost is equal to marginal revenue in all market structures.

The marginal cost curve, derived from the extra amount it takes to make one more piece of product, ends up being the supply curve in all industries. Marginal revenue is the amount of extra revenue obtained for selling the next piece of product. Only in a pure competitive market will this be equal to the price, because another unique characteristic of this structure is a supplier can supply as much as they want at the price the market sets overall. In every other market structure, to sell more product the producer must drop their price. This means the extra amount from the next sale is always less than the previous piece of product.

Why do we talk about an industry that does not exist? It is the goal for us to strive for because the more competition the better off the consumer will be in the long run. This is the only perfect market; all other structures are considered imperfect. Let's look at those structures now.

Monopoly

Monopolies have only one seller and face a demand that represents the normal law of demand, requiring them to drop prices if they want to sell more product. Other characteristics of this industry are that they have a unique product, control over their price, and power to make sure no other companies enter. Although they don't have direct competitors, monopolies do not necessarily charge the highest prices possible. However, without competition, they also fail to reach equilibrium and efficiency. This means that consumers end up paying more for the product than they would in a competitive market and the amount for sale ends up being less also.

These companies have a product that no one else is selling like, for example, your local power company. A power company is regulated by the government, so they are not a true monopoly. In fact, in the US it is illegal to have an industry with only one unregulated suppliers due to anti-trust laws. This started with the Sherman Anti-Trust Act[1] of the 1800's and continued with many other laws through the 1900's.

Understanding these market structures aids in shaping and improving real-world marketplaces, fostering competitive environments and ensuring efficient resource allocation.

---

1. U.S. Congress. *Sherman Antitrust Act*, 26 Stat. 209 (1890), codified as amended at 15 U.S.C. §§ 1–7.

Oligopoly & Monopolistic Competition

Purely competitive and monopolistic industries are mostly theoretical and do not exist in the US. They are studied to understand market extremes, providing perspective to real-world markets. Monopolistic competition and oligopolies, influenced and compared by these theoretical models, help in analyzing practical market scenarios

Oligopolies consist of a few sellers with similar products. Since there are only a few firms, they have more control over the market. These companies have power in the industry that prevents others from entering to compete. A good example of this would be the big three cell phone companies. While we do see smaller companies leasing their towers, the top three are in firm control of the market. I will admit this is one of the harder industries to model, because there are several things going on with the competition that makes it hard for economists to apply only one theory. Therefore, we end up with many theories competing to describe the market's actions. There is competition, but not enough to drive us to the point of efficiency that a pure competitive market reaches.

Despite competition, oligopolies can collude, although this practice is illegal in the United States. Collusion, aimed at setting higher prices, is prohibited to maintain competitive pricing. Even with the laws in place, companies still have tried to collude. One such case was in the 1950's and 60's when several large firms that made electrical equipment used the phases of the moon to submit bids. Each phase was assigned to a different company and during that phase the others would bid extremely high to allow the winning bid to be profitable.[2]

The most famous collusion is in the form of a cartel called OPEC (Organization of the Petroleum Exporting Countries). This organization operates outside of the US and therefore it is legal. OPEC controls the supply of oil by its members to then control price. I am sure when I used the word cartel your mind went to the drug cartels. Yes, that would also be in the realm of economics since these cartels are an oligopoly of suppliers controlling a market.

2. **United States v. General Electric Co., et al., 209 F. Supp. 197 (E.D. Pa. 1962)** (criminal antitrust prosecution of electrical equipment manufacturers for conspiracy to fix prices and rig bids in government and utility procurements).

I would argue that Monopolies and Oligopolies are bad for consumers, since both lead to higher prices and smaller supplies of goods and services. Monopolistic competition is the last structure and one we see many times in the economy. This structure involves many producers, but not as many as in purely competitive markets. Producers in this market have limited control over prices, as they sell products similar to each other. The competition forces them to adjust prices. However, they do not reach equilibrium since there are product differences and still small to medium barriers to firms entering the market. Profit maximization occurs when marginal revenue equals marginal cost, but it doesn't align with equilibrium (intersection of buyer's and seller's choices). However, the more competition there is, the closer the market gets to efficiency.

Monopolistic competition, I believe, is what the markets should try to achieve. This is another area where math and graphs help flesh out the specifics but suffice it to say that competition leads to lower prices and more supply of a good or service. Both outcomes help consumers and makes firms more honest if they want to keep your business. It also squeezes out the extra profit (economic profit) we spoke of in last chapter, which should be the goal of any market and/or government agency.

Discussion Questions

1. Why do economists study a **purely competitive market** even though it does not really exist in the real world? How does it help us understand real industries?
2. According to the chapter, why do monopolies lead to higher prices and lower output than more competitive markets? How does this affect consumers?
3. **In an oligopoly, companies may be tempted to collude even though it is illegal.** Why do you think firms still try to do this, like in the electrical equipment case from the 1950s and 1960s?
4. Why is OPEC an oligopoly, and why is it able to control oil prices even though price fixing is illegal in the United States?
5. **The chapter argues that monopolistic competition is the best structure for consumers.** Do you agree or disagree? Use examples like restaurants, clothing brands, or trade companies to support your answer.

13 Resources

This chapter briefly looks into the resource market within the circular flow model. While similar principles of supply and demand apply to both the product and resource markets, the key difference lies in the origin of resource demand, which is derived from the demand for goods and services in the product market. Here's a concise overview of the different types of resources and the corresponding payments in the resource market:

Land

Land refers to natural resources and raw materials used in production. This can be land but includes anything that comes naturally from the land: petroleum, diamonds, water, gold, and trees just to name a few. For some of these to be used, it may need one or more of the other resources to access it.

In economics, the payment made for the use of land is termed rent. Due to its fixed and scarce nature, the price for land usage depends on the scarcity of the resources needed for production. The location of the resource will also affect the cost.

Labor

Labor represents the workforce of the country. As mentioned early, this is anyone working or actively looking for a job. As you dig deeper, it becomes obvious that the type of labor can be very specialized, therefore payment will have a big range. Doctors, pilots and attorneys have a long timeline of training so they will demand a higher payment than someone that needs less training. The supply of labor will also impact the payment, and we are seeing a shortage in trade positions in the US, causing higher payments for those positions. Though a good tradesman will also need training.

My dad, who was a plumber, used to tell this story. "A homeowner calls a plumber to come fix some pipes in the basement that are rattling. The plumber goes down and listens, finds the rattling, takes out a hammer and pounds a spot. The plumber comes back up and hands a bill to the homeowner for $125. The homeowner gets upset and asks why they were being charged $125 for hitting a pipe. The plumber says that only $25 was for hitting the pipe, the other $100 was for knowing where to hit it." Knowledge and training are important; there needs to be a time in everyone's life where they stop getting paid for what they do and start getting paid for what they know.

Wages are the payment for the use of labor. Wages are essential to compensate individuals for their time and effort. The concept of trade-offs and opportunity cost, discussed earlier in the book, plays a crucial role in determining wages, as individuals weigh the value of their time against other potential activities.

Capital

Capital encompasses man-made products used in the production of goods and services. Acquiring capital often involves monetary transactions, sometimes necessitating borrowing funds. Consequently, the payment for capital usage is referred to as interest. Capital investments are crucial for businesses and require financial considerations for their utilization.

Entrepreneurship

Entrepreneurship involves the organization and coordination of the other resources. Land, labor, and capital are considered costs of doing business. After covering all these costs, what remains is profit. Profits are distributed to the shareholders in the business, which can include sole providers, partners, or shareholders. Profit serves as a return on investment, reflecting the rewards for the risks taken and successful management of the business.

In summary, the resource market involves the payment of rent for land, wages for labor, interest for capital, and profits for entrepreneurship. These payments represent the income side of the circular flow model, aligning with the income approach in calculating GDP. Understanding the dynamics of the resource market provides valuable insights into the functioning of economies and businesses.

Discussion Questions

1. Why is the demand for resources called "derived demand," and how does it connect to the demand for goods and services in the product market?
2. How do scarcity and location affect the rent paid for land and natural resources? Can you think of a real-world example where this happens?
3. In the plumber story, what does it show about how training and knowledge affect wages? How does this relate to different types of jobs in today's economy?
4. Why do businesses have to pay interest for using capital, and how does borrowing money help or hurt a business?
5. How do profits reward entrepreneurs for risk, and why are profits important for keeping businesses running and growing?

14 Last Thoughts

We have covered a lot in this book, everything from production cost and structures of markets to different types of economic systems, the indicators, business cycle, fiscal and monetary policy. I hope it has given you clear insight into the world of economics. But please understand I have very much oversimplified the discipline just so you could start to understand more complex issues. With that said, I do think the basics of economics have been lost to the general public and that is why I wrote this book. I believe that everyone needs to know the foundation of this social science. I thought I would take this last chapter to expand on some of the things we did talk about just to kind of put it in context of the real world.

We started off by talking about the very important concept of opportunity cost, which I think many people in society have lost sight of. It's the simple idea, that every time we make a choice, we give up the opportunity to make a different choice. I think that alone can put many things into context as we look across the entire economy. As we talked about earlier in the book, we only have so many resources that we can make things with, and we cannot produce everything that everybody wants. Therefore, we have to make choices in times of scarcity with the resources that we do have, this is the very basis of economics itself. Now we could spend hours talking about the different schools of thoughts and what they think is the most important. You will hear the talking heads on TV only coming from a few schools, but at the end of the day most of them have lost sight of what the everyday person goes through when they're making these choices.

We talked about a topic that's very much in the news today and that is command systems versus free markets. Or using the common term socialism versus capitalism, we see many of the younger generation buying into the idea that government can do things better for us. I would just invite anyone to look and tell me where government has, in the long run, made things better. Again, we could go through lots of different talking points here but suffice it to say that usually when the government puts its hand into a market things just get worse over time, though you may see some improvement in the short term. It's an idea that I've heard from several economists, how can we expect to put another entity into the mix, such as in healthcare, and expect prices to go down. That's just not how things work in the real world, and you can see that from real life. When fixing something at your house, the more people you call in the more costly it will be in the long run. I believe that if people will just take the time to learn about economics and see how this allocation of resources happens, this discussion between capitalism and socialism would go away fairly quickly. We don't want an oligopoly or a monopoly running anything, that would include the government running any industry. A good example is the post office, the only real mail company in the US and they lose billions of dollars a year. We do have a mixed market in the United States and will never be a free market completely. However just because we do have some public goods, like public school and libraries, that does not make us a socialist nation it just makes us a mixed economy like we discussed earlier in the book. Again, a misunderstanding by the general public about how economics works.

We can apply the things we learned about the macro economy with the aggregate supply/aggregate demand model coupling together with the inflation indicator and discuss what happened during COVID, or at least I should say what came to a climax during COVID. You can actually go back to the Great Recession of 2008 and look at the FED's policy of keeping the interest rate too low for too long. Couple this together with the crash of GDP during the beginning of COVID and the government trying to spend our way out of that recession and you get what happened with the spike of inflation during the early 2020s. If you remember in the book we spoke of demand side inflation and supply side inflation, both of which happened during that time period to push us to the highest inflation we've seen since the 1980s. We saw too much money in the system and at the same time we saw our supply chain falter. Both led to rising cost that ended up hurting not only the poorest among us but also anyone who was purchasing products during that time. At the time I am writing this book, we are still feeling the effects of those policies by the federal government and the Fed.

What happens from here? I don't think anyone can predict that especially an economist. A famous economist once said that we're not very good at predicting what's coming next, and that's true. But we can see what is being indicated or heading our way. And unless the government, again not only federal but also local and state, learn about the science of economics, I'm afraid that the future does not look bright. For them to learn about it must start with the people who elect them, so I hope this book will help people learn that economics is about everyday living. For the common sense that comes from economics to work its way up through our society and government, it must start with individuals. I hope that this book may be the start of that movement.

Thank you for taking the time for this book, I would love to hear from you!
Wes Clark, Professor of Economics

wes.the.economist@gmail.com
@westheeconomist on Facebook, Instagram and X
EconSense Podcast - Spotify, Apple and Youtube

www.ingramcontent.com/pod-product-compliance
Lightning Source LLC
LaVergne TN
LVHW050828061126
851857LV00012B/1028
9798319716194